Advanced Mathematical Team Races

Seventeen ready-to-use activities to make learning more effective and more engaging!

Paul Hambleton

Tarquin Group
www.tarquingroup.com

ALSO AVAILABLE, THE FIRST BOOK IN THIS SERIES:

Mathematical Team Races
Activities for ages 13-16
A team race is a classic idea - your team wins by answering all the questions correctly in the fastest time! Students enjoy the activity immensely and the quality of learning and discussion taking place is very high.

The element of competition means students must answer questions as quickly as possible, but accuracy is also essential as students need correct answers in order to progress and win the race. Student feedback is excellent.

This first book has been well received in a wide variety of schools.
ISBN 978 1 90755 021 8

Advanced Mathematical Team Races
© Paul Hambleton 2015

ISBN 978 1 90755 022 5

Tarquin,
Suite 74 Holywell Hill
St Albans AL1 1DT
UK

www.tarquingroup.com

Distributed and printed in the USA by
IPG Books www.ipgbook.com available
www.amazon.com & major retailers

Distributed in Australia by OLM www.lat-olm.com.au

A catalogue record for this book is available from the British Library.
Printed in the UK, Australia and USA.

Introduction

A team race is a classic idea (your team wins by answering all the questions correctly in the fastest time!) that I used in a lesson once and it worked so well it became something I did whenever that topic came up, as students enjoyed the activity so much, and I felt the quality of learning and discussion taking place was very high. This second book in the series contains activities based on Advanced Level core mathematics content. It can be incredibly difficult to find interesting resources as alternatives to a textbook, yet I have found that post-16 students enjoy these activities just as much as younger ones and they are just as effective in developing their learning. They still enjoy the competitive nature of the activities and they promote rich discussions in overcoming misconceptions when tackling the problems in small groups.

How to organise a team race

Decide what size teams you would like students to be in. Pairs works very well, giving students enough to do, but larger teams can work well too. The number of teams you decide on is the number of copies of the photocopiable card page you will need. Cut out the cards and arrange into stacks of Round 1, Round 2, etc. in front of you. Give each team the card with Round 1 on it. You may prefer to place these face down and get students to turn them over at the same time, which can help to create a buzz about the activity.

Students then answer the question on Round 1, and when they have an answer they present the answer to you (ensuring they don't allow other pairs or groups to see the answer). You may like to get students to write answers on paper, in books, or on mini-whiteboards. If the answer is correct, give them Round 2, and this continues until the first pair or group has completed all the rounds you wish them to complete. It may be necessary to offer some quiet support to some pairs or groups if they are struggling on a particular round, otherwise they may become stuck and despondent. The winning pair or group is the first to complete all rounds.

You don't have to use all 10 rounds. The questions are written with the intention that in general, each round is more difficult than the last. So you can have a quick glance at the questions and decide which rounds you want to use in your team race. You may miss off the first few if they are too easy, or the last few if they are too difficult.

You may wish to print the cards on coloured card or laminate them to make them more durable. Once copied, as long as you don't allow students to write on the cards, they can be used again and again, and the activity is very simple to set up, as the cards and something to write with are the only resources you need.

Answers

An answer sheet is provided for each of the pre-prepared activities. Make sure students can't see these!

Active learning

Active learning strategies are becoming ever more popular in schools wishing to give students not only a more enjoyable experience but also a deeper understanding of mathematics through collaborative learning and more independent learning, and this type of activity can encourage this.

Differentiation

These activities are easy to differentiate. You can miss off later, more difficult rounds as appropriate to the ability of your students, or you can easily make up some more challenging questions to tack on as additional rounds at the end. In particular often the last few rounds include worded questions, where students have to interpret the question and use the skills developed in an earlier part of the race to answer them. As this is a collaborative activity, students will be able to support each other.

Make your own versions

Once you have used some of the pre-prepared sets of cards, you may wish to create your own versions. There is a blank template provided for this purpose.

Which topics does this work well for?

Team races work well for topics which require some degree of working out to be done by students, for two reasons. Firstly for the activity to work well, the teacher needs to check each answer, and so there should be enough work on each question to keep students busy for a few minutes. Secondly, this idea promotes collaborative working and multi-stage questions are ideally suited to this.

Race 1: Midpoints, Gradients and Distances

AS/A2 Level	TOPICS
AS	*applying the midpoint formula* *applying the gradient formula* *applying the distance formula*

TEACHER'S NOTES

Once students are aware of the formulae for calculating the midpoint and gradient of, and distance between, two points on a co-ordinate grid, they can use this activity to ensure they can apply the formulae accurately.

ANSWERS

Round 1	Round 2
(3,5.5)	-4

Round 3	Round 4
$\sqrt{32} \approx 5.66$	Gradient: 1 Midpoint: (3,9)

Round 5	Round 6
Midpoint: (1,6) Distance: $\sqrt{65} \approx 8.06$	Gradient: $\frac{1}{2}$ Midpoint: (1,–2) Distance: $\sqrt{20} \approx 4.47$

Round 7	Round 8
(0,–4)	$\sqrt{80} \approx 8.94$

Round 9	Round 10
$y = 3x - 4$	(5,6) or (7,10)

You may wish to specify beforehand whether you would like students to give surd answers in exact form, or whether you will accept decimal equivalents. Decimal equivalents have been given correct to 2 decimal places.

 **Round 1**

 **Round 2**

Find the coordinates of the midpoint of the line segment between the points (1,2) and (5,9)

Find the gradient of the line which goes through the points (6,11)and (8,3)

 **Round 3**

 **Round 4**

Find the distance between the points (8,3) and (12,7)

What is the gradient and midpoint of the line segment joining the points (−2,4) and (8,14)?

 **Round 5**

 **Round 6**

What is the midpoint of the line between (−6,2) and (8,10)? What is the distance from the midpoint to one of the end points?

(−1,−3) and (3,−1)
What is the gradient and midpoint of the line segment joining the two points?
How far apart are the two points?

 **Round 7**

 **Round 8**

The midpoint of a particular line segment is (15,−1). One end point is (3,2). What are the co-ordinates of the other end point?

The midpoint of a line segment is (−4,3) and one end point is (−8,5). What is the length of the line segment?

 **Round 9**

 **Round 10**

(0,−4) and (5,11) are two points on a line. What is the equation of the line? Give your answer in the form $y = mx + c$.

(6,8) is one end of a line segment which has gradient 2, and the length of the line segment is $\sqrt{5}$ units. What are the co-ordinates of the two possible other end points of the line segment?
Hint: Can you form a pair of simultaneous equations using the distance and gradient formulae?

Race 2: Factorising and Solving Cubic Equations

AS/A2 Level	TOPICS
AS	*factorising a cubic expression* *solving cubic equations* *applying the Factor theorem*

TEACHER'S NOTES

This race is all about using the factor theorem to factorise cubic expressions. It also extends to finding solutions of cubic equations.

ANSWERS

Round 1	Round 2
$(x-2)(x+3)(x+4)$	$(x-5)(x+1)(x+2)$

Round 3	Round 4
$(x-3)(x+3)(x+4)$	$(x-3)(x+2)(x+6)$

Round 5	Round 6
$x = -2\ -1\ or\ 1$	$x = 3, 4\ or\ 5$

Round 7	Round 8
$(x-1)^2(x+6)$	$(x+1)(x+2)(x+3)$

Round 9	Round 10
$x = -3, -2\ or\ 1$	$x = -2\ or\ 2$

Round 1

 Round 2

Factorise
$$x^3 + 5x^2 - 2x - 24,$$
given that $(x - 2)$ is a factor.

Factorise
$$x^3 - 2x^2 - 13x - 10,$$
given that $(x + 1)$ is a factor.

 Round 3

 Round 4

$$f(x) = x^3 + 4x^2 - 9x - 36$$
$$f(3) = 0$$
Factorise $f(x)$ fully.

$$f(x) = x^3 + 5x^2 - 12x - 36$$
$$f(-2) = 0$$
Factorise $f(x)$ fully.

 Round 5

 Round 6

$$f(x) = x^3 + 2x^2 - x - 2$$
$$f(1) = 0$$
Solve $f(x) = 0$.

$$f(x) = x^3 - 12x^2 + 47x - 60$$
$$f(5) = 0$$
Solve $f(x) = 0$.

 Round 7

 Round 8

$$f(x) = x^3 + 4x^2 - 11x + 6$$
Factorise $f(x)$ fully.

$$f(x) = x^3 + 6x^2 + 11x + 6$$
Factorise $f(x)$ fully.

 Round 9

 Round 10

Solve
$$x^3 + 4x^2 + x - 6 = 0$$

Solve
$$x^3 + 2x^2 - 4x - 8 = 0$$

Race 3: The Binomial Expansion

AS/A2 Level	TOPICS
AS/A2	*expanding binomial expressions*

TEACHER'S NOTES

This activity could be used to develop understanding of the Binomial expansion at AS-level, by just using the first 8 cards. Alternatively it could be used as a recap for A2 students before tackling the last 2 cards, one of which has a negative power and one has a fractional power.

ANSWERS

Round 1	Round 2
$1+10x+40x^2+80x^3+80x^4+32x^5$	$1-12x+48x^2-64x^3$

Round 3	Round 4
$1+6x+15x^2+20x^3+15x^4+6x^5+x^6$	$81x^4+216x^3+216x^2+96x+16$

Round 5	Round 6
1792	14,080

Round 7	Round 8
-4032	70

Round 9	Round 10
$1-6x+27x^2-108x^3$	$1+x-\dfrac{x^2}{2}+\dfrac{x^3}{2}$

Round 1

Expand

$$(1+2x)^5$$

Round 2

Expand

$$(1-4x)^3$$

Round 3

Expand

$$(1+x)^6$$

Round 4

Expand

$$(3x+2)^4$$

Round 5

Find the coefficient of x^6 in the expansion of

$$(2x+1)^8$$

Round 6

Find the coefficient of x^3 in the expansion of

$$(1+4x)^{12}$$

Round 7

Find the coefficient of x^5 in the expansion of

$$(1-2x)^9$$

Round 8

Find the value of the constant term in the expansion of

$$\left(x+\frac{1}{x}\right)^8$$

Round 9

Find the first four terms in the expansion of

$$(1+3x)^{-2}$$

Round 10

Find the first four terms in the expansion of

$$(1+2x)^{\frac{1}{2}}$$

Race 4: Arithmetic Sequences and Series

AS/A2 Level	TOPICS
AS	finding a specific term in an arithmetic sequence finding the sum of an arithmetic sequence deducing the first term and common difference when given two terms solving problems involving arithmetic sequences

TEACHER'S NOTES

This activity starts with some basic calculations using formulae associated with arithmetic sequences and series, before giving students the chance to tackle more exam-style questions where they are given abstract bits of information which they have to use to determine a and/or d.

ANSWERS

Round 1	Round 2
77	−292

Round 3	Round 4
730	25050

Round 5	Round 6
First term: 6 Common difference: 3	−296

Round 7	Round 8
First term: 5 Common difference: 4	£185

Round 9	Round 10
£100	£630

Round 1

5 is the first term of an arithmetic sequence which has common difference 3. Using the formula
$$a_n = a + (n-1)d$$
find the 25th term in the sequence.

 Round 2

2 is the first term of an arithmetic sequence which has common difference -6. Using the formula
$$a_n = a + (n-1)d$$
find the 50th term in the sequence.

 Round 3

A sequence starts with the number 8 and each term is 3 greater than the previous one. Using the formula
$$S_n = \frac{n}{2}\left(2a + (n-1)d\right)$$
find the sum of the first 20 terms in the sequence.

 Round 4

A sequence starts with the number 3 and each term is 5 more than the previous one. Using the formula
$$S_n = \frac{n}{2}\left(2a + (n-1)d\right)$$
find the sum of the first 100 terms in the sequence.

 Round 5

The 10th term in an arithmetic sequence is 33 and the 20th term is 63.
Find the first term in the sequence and the common difference between each term.

 Round 6

The 20th term in an arithmetic sequence is -56 and the 26th term is -74.

Find the 100th term in the sequence.

 Round 7

The 10th term of an arithmetic sequence is 41, and the sum of the first 10 terms is 230.
Find the first term in the sequence and the common difference between each term.

 Round 8

Henry's grandmother puts £100 into a savings account for him on the day he is born. Each year on his birthday she puts in £5 more than she did the previous year. How much does she pay into the account on his 18th birthday?

 Round 9

A quiz of 10 questions awards a £2 prize for the first question correct, £5 for the second, £8 for the third, and so on. The first time a question is answered incorrectly, the quiz stops but the player keeps all money won so far. What is the value of the prize if a person answers the ninth question incorrectly?

 Round 10

When Hayley is 10 she starts putting birthday money into a piggy bank. When she is 14 she puts in £70 and when she is 18 she puts in £110. The amount she receives increases by the same amount each year. Assuming she doesn't spend any of the money, how much will she have in her piggy bank after her 18th birthday?

Race 5: Geometric Sequences and Series

AS/A2 Level	TOPICS
AS	finding a specific term in a geometric sequence finding the sum of a geometric sequence deducing the first term and common ratio when given two terms solving problems involving geometric sequences

TEACHER'S NOTES

This activity starts with some basic calculations using formulae associated with geometric sequences and series, before giving students the chance to tackle more exam-style questions where they are given abstract bits of information which they have to use to determine a and/or r.

ANSWERS

Round 1	Round 2
13,122	0.012

Round 3	Round 4
82	49

Round 5	Round 6
First term: 2 Common ratio: 4	0.9375

Round 7	Round 8
150	£262,144

Round 9	Round 10
£364	£1023.50

Round 1

A geometric sequence starts with the number 2. The common ratio of the sequence is 3.

Using the formula $a_n = ar^{n-1}$, find the value of the 9th term.

Round 2

The first term of a sequence is 6. Each term is half the value of the previous term.

Using the formula $a_n = ar^{n-1}$, find the value of the 10th term. Round your answer to 3 decimal places.

Round 3

The first term of a geometric sequence is 5, and the common ratio is 1.2.

Using the formula $S_n = \dfrac{a(r^n - 1)}{r - 1}$, find the sum of the first 8 terms of the sequence. Round your answer to the nearest whole number.

Round 4

A geometric sequence has first term 20 and common ratio 0.6.

Using the formula $S_n = \dfrac{a(1 - r^n)}{1 - r}$, find the sum of the first 8 terms of the sequence. Round your answer to the nearest whole number.

Round 5

The 3rd term of a geometric sequence is 32 and the 5th term is 512.

Find the first term and common ratio of the sequence.

Round 6

The 4th term of a geometric sequence is 30 and the 7th term is 3.75.

What is the 9th term?

Round 7

The 5th term of a geometric sequence is 160 and the 8th term is 1280.

Find the sum of the first 4 terms.

Round 8

Laura's grandfather puts £2 into a savings account for her first birthday. Each year on her birthday he puts in twice as much as he did the previous year. If he continued in this way, how much would he have to pay into the account on Laura's 18th birthday?

Round 9

A game show consists of a quiz of 10 questions, and a £1 prize is awarded for answering the first question correctly, and the prize for each subsequent question is three times the prize of the previous one. The first time a question is answered incorrectly, the quiz stops but the player keeps all money won so far. What is the value of the prize if a person answers the seventh question incorrectly?

Round 10

When Jason is 8 he starts putting birthday money into a piggy bank. When he is 13 he puts in £16 and when he is 18 he puts in £512. The amount he receives each year forms a geometric sequence. Assuming he doesn't spend any of the money, how much will he have in his piggy bank after his 18th birthday?

Race 6: Differentiating Using Standard Results

AS/A2 Level	TOPICS
AS	differentiating polynomials differentiating negative powers of x differentiating fractional powers of x

TEACHER'S NOTES

This race will get students differentiating polynomials using standard results. The last two cards, while containing expressions which aren't strictly polynomials, will give students the chance to use negative and fractional powers, if you so wish. You could easily replace the last 2 cards with proper polynomials to make it easier, or you could replace earlier cards with more expressions containing negative or fractional powers, to make it more difficult.

ANSWERS

Round 1	Round 2
1	0

Round 3	Round 4
$6x + 5$	$6x^5 - 8x^3 + 18x$

Round 5	Round 6
35	-14

Round 7	Round 8
$-2x^{-3} + 12x^2$	$\dfrac{1}{2}x^{-\frac{1}{2}} + 6$

Round 9	Round 10
$-15x^{-4}$	3

	Round 1		Round 2

$y = x + 4$

Find $\dfrac{dy}{dx}$.

$y = 2$

Find $\dfrac{dy}{dx}$.

	Round 3		Round 4

$y = 3x^2 + 5x - 2$

Find $\dfrac{dy}{dx}$.

$y = x^6 - 2x^4 + 9x^2 + 1$

Find $\dfrac{dy}{dx}$.

	Round 5		Round 6

What is the gradient of the line with equation $y = 5x^7 - 2$ at the point where $x = 1$?

What is the gradient of the line with equation $y = 4x^2 + 2x - 3$ at the point where $x = -2$?

	Round 7		Round 8

$y = x^{-2} + 4x^3 - 2$

Find $\dfrac{dy}{dx}$.

$y = x^{\frac{1}{2}} + 6x + 4$

Find $\dfrac{dy}{dx}$.

	Round 9		Round 10

$y = \dfrac{5}{x^3}$

Find $\dfrac{dy}{dx}$.

What is the gradient of the line with equation $y = 4x^{\frac{1}{2}} + 2x$ at the point where $x = 4$?

Race 7: Straight Lines, Tangents and Normals

AS/A2 Level	TOPICS
AS	*finding the equation of a straight line given two points on the line* *finding the equation of the tangent at a given point* *finding the equation of the normal at a given point*

TEACHER'S NOTES

The main skill in this race is the ability to find the equations of tangents and normals. The activity starts with substituting into and rearranging the general equation of a straight line given two points on the line, or given one point and the line's gradient. This race will develop their speed and accuracy in using this result, and this is also good revision of the gradient formula.

ANSWERS

Round 1	Round 2
$y = 6x - 29$	$y = 3x - 5$

Round 3	Round 4
$2x + y = 4$	$y = \dfrac{4}{3}x + \dfrac{13}{3}$

Round 5	Round 6
$y = 6x - 5$	$x + 4y = 34$

Round 7	Round 8
$24x + y + 28 = 0$	$8x + y = 3$

Round 9	Round 10
$x + 30y + 933 = 0$	$x + 19y - 993 = 0$

 **Round 1**

A line has gradient 6 and goes through the point (5,1). What is the equation of the line?

Give your answer in the form $y = mx + c$.

 **Round 2**

What is the equation of the line which goes through the points (2,1) and (5,10)?

Give your answer in the form $y = mx + c$.

 **Round 3**

What is the equation of the line which goes through (−1,6) and (6,−8)?

Give your answer in the form $ax + by = c$.

 **Round 4**

What is the equation of the line which goes through (2,7) and (8,15)?

Give your answer in the form $y = mx + c$.

 **Round 5**

Find the equation of the tangent to the curve

$y = x^2 + 4$ at the point where $x = 3$.

Give your answer in the form $y = mx + c$.

 **Round 6**

Find the equation of the normal to the curve

$y = x^2 + 4$ at the point where $x = 2$.

Give your answer in the form $ax + by = c$.

 **Round 7**

Find the equation of the tangent to the curve

$y = 5x^2 - 4x - 8$ at the point where $x = -2$.

Give your answer in the form $ax + by + c = 0$.

 **Round 8**

Find the equation of the tangent to the curve

$y = 2x^3 - 7x^2$ at the point where $x = 1$.

Give your answer in the form $ax + by = c$.

 **Round 9**

Find the equation of the normal to the curve

$y = x^3 + 3x + 5$ at the point where $x = -3$.

Give your answer in the form $ax + by + c = 0$.

 **Round 10**

Find the equation of the normal to the curve

$y = 2x^2 - x + 7$ at the point where $x = 5$.

Give your answer in the form $ax + by + c = 0$.

Race 8: Integrating Using Standard Results

AS/A2 Level	TOPICS
AS	integrating polynomials integrating negative powers of x, except -1 integrating fractional powers of x

TEACHER'S NOTES

This race will get students practising integrating using standard results, and it will enable them to apply integration to solving problems such as finding the equation of a line and finding areas.

ANSWERS

Round 1	Round 2
$x^2 + 3x + c$	$\dfrac{9}{4}$
Round 3	**Round 4**
2.75	$\dfrac{x^6}{6} - x^4 + x^2 + c$
Round 5	**Round 6**
$y = x^2 + x + 2$	$y = x^3 + \dfrac{x^2}{2} - 5x + 16$
Round 7	**Round 8**
$4\dfrac{2}{3}$ square units	4.5 square units
Round 9	**Round 10**
$\dfrac{2}{3}x^{\frac{3}{2}} + \dfrac{5x^2}{2} + c$	1

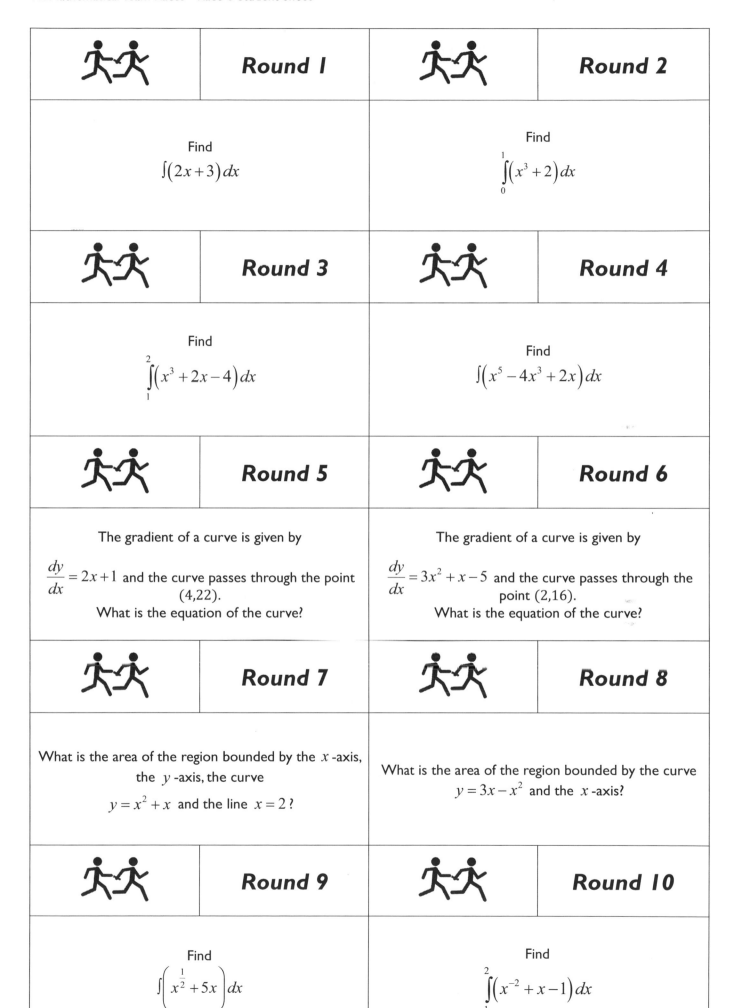 **Round 1**	**Round 2**
Find $$\int (2x+3)\,dx$$	Find $$\int_{0}^{1} (x^3+2)\,dx$$

Round 3	**Round 4**
Find $$\int_{1}^{2} (x^3+2x-4)\,dx$$	Find $$\int (x^5-4x^3+2x)\,dx$$

Round 5	**Round 6**
The gradient of a curve is given by $\dfrac{dy}{dx}=2x+1$ and the curve passes through the point (4,22). What is the equation of the curve?	The gradient of a curve is given by $\dfrac{dy}{dx}=3x^2+x-5$ and the curve passes through the point (2,16). What is the equation of the curve?

Round 7	**Round 8**
What is the area of the region bounded by the x-axis, the y-axis, the curve $y=x^2+x$ and the line $x=2$?	What is the area of the region bounded by the curve $y=3x-x^2$ and the x-axis?

Round 9	**Round 10**
Find $$\int \left(x^{\frac{1}{2}}+5x \right) dx$$	Find $$\int_{1}^{2} (x^{-2}+x-1)\,dx$$

Race 9: Simplifying Logarithmic Expressions

AS/A2 Level	TOPICS
A2	*applying the laws of logarithms* *simplifying expressions using the laws of logarithms*

TEACHER'S NOTES

This race will enable students to apply their understanding of the laws of logarithms.

ANSWERS

Round 1	Round 2
3	7

Round 3	Round 4
$\log 10$	$\log 27$

Round 5	Round 6
$\log \dfrac{1}{2}$	$\log 9$

Round 7	Round 8
$7 \log x$	$4 \log x$

Round 9	Round 10
$\log(108x^5)$	$2x$

Round 1

Without a calculator, evaluate

$$\log_4 64$$

Round 2

Without a calculator, evaluate

$$\log_2 128$$

Round 3

Write the following expression as a single logarithm:

$$\log 100 - \log 10$$

Round 4

Write the following expression as a single logarithm:

$$\log 3 + \log 9$$

Round 5

Write the following in terms of $\log x$, where x is a number:

$$\log x^2 + 5 \log x$$

Round 6

Write the following in terms of $\log x$, where x is a number:

$$\frac{1}{2} \log 81$$

Round 7

Express the following in terms of $\log x$:

$$\log x^2 + 5 \log x$$

Round 8

Express the following in terms of $\log x$:

$$6 \log x - \log x^2$$

Round 9

Simplify the following expression:

$$2 \log 2x + 3 \log 3x$$

Round 10

What expression should replace the ? in this equation?

$$\log 8x^3 = 3 \log ?$$

Race 10: Partial Fractions

AS/A2 Level	TOPICS
A2	*expressing a rational function in partial fractions*

TEACHER'S NOTES

The premise of this race is simple; students need to know how to split an algebraic fraction into partial fractions.

ANSWERS

Round 1	Round 2
$$\frac{1}{x+2}+\frac{1}{x+3}$$	$$\frac{1}{5(x-1)}+\frac{4}{5(x+4)}$$

Round 3	Round 4
$$\frac{2}{x+2}-\frac{1}{x+1}$$	$$\frac{9}{x+3}-\frac{3}{x-4}$$

Round 5	Round 6
$$\frac{1}{x^2}+\frac{1}{x+1}-\frac{1}{x}$$	$$\frac{2x+1}{x^2+3}+\frac{5}{x-6}$$

Round 7	Round 8
$$\frac{3}{x-1}+\frac{1}{x+2}+\frac{1}{x-2}$$	$$\frac{12}{5(x-7)}-\frac{2}{5(x+3)}$$

Round 9	Round 10
$$\frac{2}{2x-1}+\frac{1}{x+3}$$	$$\frac{2x}{x^2+1}-\frac{1}{x-5}$$

Round 1

Express

$$\frac{2x+5}{(x+2)(x+3)}$$

in partial fractions.

 Round 2

Express

$$\frac{x}{x^2+3x-4}$$

in partial fractions.

 Round 3

Express

$$\frac{x^2+x}{(x+1)^2(x+2)}$$

in partial fractions.

 Round 4

Express

$$\frac{6x-45}{(x-4)(x+3)}$$

in partial fractions.

 Round 5

Express

$$\frac{1}{x^2(x+1)}$$

in partial fractions.

 Round 6

Express

$$\frac{7x^2-11x+9}{(x^2+3)(x-6)}$$

in partial fractions.

 Round 7

Express

$$\frac{5x^2-2x-12}{(x^2-4)(x-1)}$$

in partial fractions.

 Round 8

Express

$$\frac{2x+10}{(x+3)(x-7)}$$

in partial fractions.

 Round 9

Express

$$\frac{4x+5}{(x+3)(2x-1)}$$

in partial fractions.

 Round 10

Express

$$\frac{x^2-10x-1}{(x^2+1)(x-5)}$$

in partial fractions.

Race 11: The Chain Rule

AS/A2 Level	TOPICS
A2	*using the Chain rule to differentiate composite functions*

TEACHER'S NOTES

The questions in this race are composite functions which require the chain rule in order to be differentiated. You can be as strict as you like with the level of working you expect – you might want full working such as would be expected in an exam, or you might allow students to find answers by inspection.

ANSWERS

Round 1	Round 2
$4(2x+1)$	$15x^2(x^3-2)^4$
Round 3	**Round 4**
$2(4x+9)^{-\frac{1}{2}}$	$-21(3x-4)^{-8}$
Round 5	**Round 6**
$2x^{-\frac{1}{2}}\left(\sqrt{x}+2\right)^3$	$-6x(x^2+4)^{-4}$
Round 7	**Round 8**
$-\dfrac{18x^2}{\left(x^3+1\right)^7}$	$y=20x-19$
Round 9	**Round 10**
$6x+y=5$	10

 **Round 1**

$$y = (2x+1)^2$$

Find $\dfrac{dy}{dx}$.

 **Round 2**

$$y = (x^3 - 2)^5$$

Find $\dfrac{dy}{dx}$.

 **Round 3**

$$y = (4x+9)^{\frac{1}{2}}$$

Find $\dfrac{dy}{dx}$.

 **Round 4**

$$y = \dfrac{1}{(3x-4)^7}$$

Find $\dfrac{dy}{dx}$.

 **Round 5**

$$y = (\sqrt{x} + 2)^4$$

Find $\dfrac{dy}{dx}$.

 **Round 6**

$$y = (x^2 + 4)^{-3}$$

Find $\dfrac{dy}{dx}$.

 **Round 7**

$$y = \dfrac{1}{(x^3 + 1)^6}$$

Find $\dfrac{dy}{dx}$.

 **Round 8**

What is the equation of the tangent to the curve with equation $y = (5x-4)^4$ at the point where $x = 1$?

 **Round 9**

 **Round 10**

What is the equation of the normal to the curve with equation $y = \dfrac{1}{(x^2 - 2)^3}$ at the point where $x = 1$?

Find the gradient of the tangent to the curve with equation $y = (2x+3)^5$ at the point where $x = -1$?

Race 12: The Product and Quotient Rules

AS/A2 Level	TOPICS
A2	*using the Product rule to differentiate products* *using the Quotient rule to differentiate quotients* *determining whether the Product or Quotient rule is appropriate*

TEACHER'S NOTES

Students will need to know how to use the Product and Quotient rules. The functions which make up the products and quotients are all fairly simple to differentiate.

ANSWERS

Round 1	Round 2
$(30x+17)(2x+1)$ or $60x^2+64x+17$	$x^3(12x^2-15x+16)$ or $12x^5-15x^4+16x^3$

Round 3	Round 4
$\dfrac{3}{(2x+3)^2}$	$\dfrac{1-3x}{x^3}$

Round 5	Round 6
$\dfrac{5x^2-20}{2\sqrt{x-3}}$	$-\dfrac{2x(9x+2)}{(3x-1)^6}$

Round 7	Round 8
848	$\dfrac{1}{2}$

Round 9	Round 10
0	4352

	Round 1		**Round 2**

$$y = (5x+3)(2x+1)^2$$

Find $\dfrac{dy}{dx}$.

$$y = x^4\left(2x^2 - 3x + 4\right)$$

Find $\dfrac{dy}{dx}$.

	Round 3		**Round 4**

$$y = \frac{x}{2x+3}$$

Find $\dfrac{dy}{dx}$.

$$y = \frac{6x-1}{2x^2}$$

Find $\dfrac{dy}{dx}$.

	Round 5		**Round 6**

$$y = \sqrt{x-3}\,(x+2)^2$$

Find $\dfrac{dy}{dx}$.

$$y = \frac{2x^2}{(3x-1)^5}$$

Find $\dfrac{dy}{dx}$.

	Round 7		**Round 8**

$$y = \left(2x^3 + 5x\right)(3x-1)^4$$

Find the gradient of the tangent to the graph of y when $x = 1$.

$$y = \frac{x}{(x+3)^2}$$

Find the gradient of the tangent to the graph of y when $x = -1$.

	Round 9		**Round 10**

$$y = \frac{2x^3}{(x-4)^5}$$

Find the gradient of the tangent to the graph of y when $x = 0$.

$$y = \left(x^4 + 1\right)(x-1)^4$$

Find the gradient of the tangent to the graph of y when $x = 3$.

Race 13: Differentiating Exponential and Natural Logarithm Functions

AS/A2 Level	TOPICS
A2	differentiating functions involving the exponential function differentiating functions involving the natural logarithm function applying the Chain, Product and Quotient rules

TEACHER'S NOTES

This race will enable students to practise differentiating exponential and natural logarithm functions. They will also need to remember how to use the Chain, Product and Quotient rules in order to differentiate.

ANSWERS

Round 1	Round 2
$2e^{2x}$	$xe^x + e^x = e^x(x+1)$

Round 3	Round 4
$(12x^2+1)e^{4x^3+x-2}$	$6xe^{x^2}$

Round 5	Round 6
$\dfrac{4}{4x+1}$	$\dfrac{2x-5}{x^2-5x}$

Round 7	Round 8
$-e^{-2x}(2x-1)$	$18e$

Round 9	Round 10
$\left(-1, \dfrac{1}{e}\right)$	$\left(\dfrac{1}{e}, -\dfrac{2}{e}\right)$ and $\left(-\dfrac{1}{e}, \dfrac{2}{e}\right)$

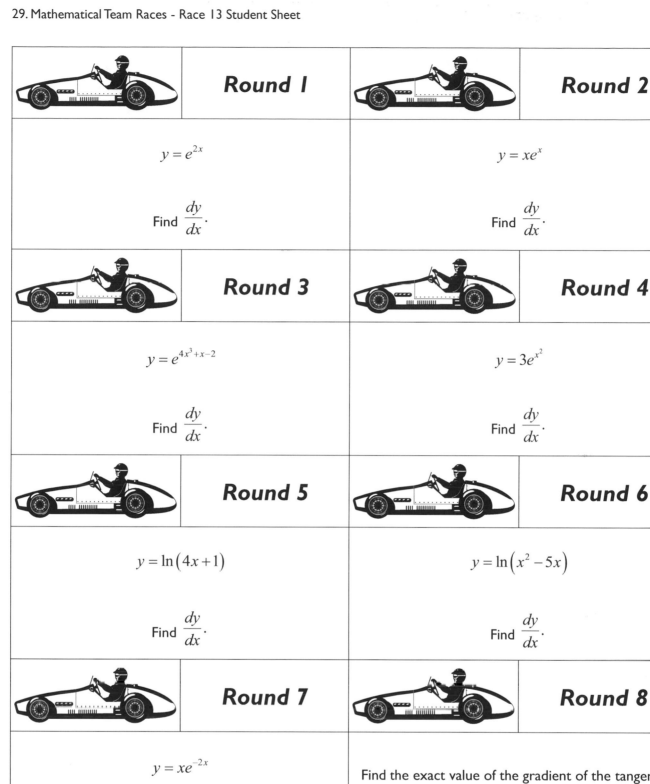

Round 1

$y = e^{2x}$

Find $\dfrac{dy}{dx}$.

Round 2

$y = xe^x$

Find $\dfrac{dy}{dx}$.

Round 3

$y = e^{4x^3 + x - 2}$

Find $\dfrac{dy}{dx}$.

Round 4

$y = 3e^{x^2}$

Find $\dfrac{dy}{dx}$.

Round 5

$y = \ln(4x + 1)$

Find $\dfrac{dy}{dx}$.

Round 6

$y = \ln(x^2 - 5x)$

Find $\dfrac{dy}{dx}$.

Round 7

$y = xe^{-2x}$

Find $\dfrac{dy}{dx}$.

Round 8

Find the exact value of the gradient of the tangent to the curve with equation $y = 3x^5 e^x$ at the point where $x = 1$.

Round 9

Find the coordinates of the stationary point on the curve with equation $y = e^{x^2 + 2x}$.

Round 10

Find the co-ordinates of the stationary points on the graph of the curve with equation $y = x\ln(x^2)$.

Race 14: Differentiating Trignometric Functions

AS/A2 Level	TOPICS
A2	*differentiating trigonometric functions* *applying the Chain, Product and Quotient rules*

TEACHER'S NOTES

This race will enable students to practise differentiating trigonometric functions. They will also need to remember how to use the Chain, Product and Quotient rules in order to differentiate.

ANSWERS

Round 1	Round 2
$5\cos(5x)$	$2x\cos(x) - x^2\sin(x)$

Round 3	Round 4
$\cos^2(x) - \sin^2(x)$	$\cos(x) - \sin(x)$

Round 5	Round 6
$\dfrac{\sin(x) - x\cos(x)}{\sin^2(x)}$	$9\sin(3x) + 4\cos(2x)$

Round 7	Round 8
$2\sin(x)\cos(x)$	$\dfrac{\pi}{4}$

Round 9	Round 10
$y = x - (\pi + 1)$	$-2e^{\pi}$

	Round 1		**Round 2**
	$y = \sin(5x)$ Find $\dfrac{dy}{dx}$.		$y = x^2 \cos(x)$ Find $\dfrac{dy}{dx}$.
	Round 3		**Round 4**
	$y = \sin(x)\cos(x)$ Find $\dfrac{dy}{dx}$.		$y = \sin(x) + \cos(x)$ Find $\dfrac{dy}{dx}$.
	Round 5		**Round 6**
	$y = \dfrac{x}{\sin(x)}$ Find $\dfrac{dy}{dx}$.		$y = 2\sin(2x) - 3\cos(3x)$ Find $\dfrac{dy}{dx}$.
	Round 7		**Round 8**
	$y = \sin^2(x)$ Find $\dfrac{dy}{dx}$.		Find the coordinates of the stationary point on the curve with equation $y = \sin(x) + \cos(x)$ for $0 < x < \dfrac{\pi}{2}$, giving your answers in terms of π.
	Round 9		**Round 10**
	Find the equation of the normal to the curve with equation $y = \dfrac{\cos(x)}{\sin(x)+1}$ the point where $x = \pi$.		Find the exact value of the gradient of the tangent to the curve with equation $y = 2\cos(x)e^x$ at the point where $x = \pi$.

Race 15: Integration by Substitution

AS/A2 Level	TOPICS
A2	*fusing integration by substitution to evaluate definite and indefinite integrals*

TEACHER'S NOTES

In all of the questions in this race, an appropriate substitution is given. Depending on your group you may wish to not give students the substitution.

ANSWERS

Round 1	Round 2
$\dfrac{(x+1)^3}{3}+c$	68.2
Round 3	**Round 4**
$\dfrac{(x^2+2)^4}{4}+c$	10.5
Round 5	**Round 6**
$\dfrac{2}{15}(x+1)^{\frac{3}{2}}(3x-2)+c$	$\dfrac{(3x^2+4x)^6}{6}+c$
Round 7	**Round 8**
$\ln\left(\dfrac{4}{3}\right)\approx 0.288$	$\ln\left(x^3-5x+3\right)+c$
Round 9	**Round 10**
$\ln\left(\dfrac{11}{3}\right)\approx 1.299$	$e^{x^2}+c$

Your students may be able to find the answers to these questions by inspection. If this is the case, you will need to specify beforehand how much, if any, working you will require to be given with the answer.

 **Round 1**

Find

$$\int (x+1)^2 \, dx$$

You may wish to use the substitution $u = x+1$

 **Round 2**

Find

$$\int_1^2 (3x-2)^4 \, dx$$

You may wish to use the substitution $u = 3x-2$

 **Round 3**

Find

$$\int 2x\left(x^2+2\right)^3 \, dx$$

You may wish to use the substitution $u = x^2+2$

 **Round 4**

Find

$$\int_0^1 4x^3\left(x^4+1\right)^5 \, dx$$

You may wish to use the substitution $u = x^4+1$

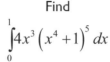 **Round 5**

Find

$$\int x\sqrt{x+1}\,dx$$

You may wish to use the substitution $u = x+1$

 Round 6

Find

$$\int (6x+4)\left(3x^2+4x\right)^5 \, dx$$

You may wish to use the substitution $u = 3x^2+4x$

 **Round 7**

Find

$$\int_0^1 \frac{2x}{x^2+3} \, dx$$

You may wish to use the substitution $u = x^2+3$

 **Round 8**

Find

$$\int \frac{3x^2-5}{x^3-5x+3} \, dx$$

You may wish to use the substitution $u = x^3-5x+3$

 **Round 9**

$$\int_2^3 \frac{2x+3}{x^2+3x-7} \, dx$$

You may wish to use the substitution $u = x^2+3x-7$

 **Round 10**

Find

$$\int 2xe^{x^2} \, dx$$

You may wish to use the substitution $u = x^2$

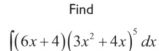

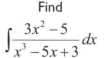

Race 16: Integration by Parts

AS/A2 Level	TOPICS
A2	*using integration by parts to evaluate definite and indefinite integrals*

TEACHER'S NOTES

All of the questions in this race require integration by parts to find the integral. There is a mixture of definite and indefinite integrals.

ANSWERS

Round 1	Round 2
0.382	$\dfrac{1}{2}x^2\ln(x)-\dfrac{1}{4}x^2+c$

Round 3	Round 4
$\sin(x)-x\cos(x)+c$	0.301

Round 5	Round 6
$\dfrac{8}{3}\ln 2-\dfrac{7}{9}$	$e^x(x-1)+c$

Round 7	Round 8
$-3e^{-x}(x+1)+c$	$\dfrac{1}{4}e^2+\dfrac{1}{4}$

Round 9	Round 10
0.562 square units	$x\ln x-x+c$

	Round 1		**Round 2**

Evaluate

$$\int_0^1 x\cos(x)\,dx$$

Give your answer correct to 3 significant figures.

$$\int x\ln(x)\,dx$$

	Round 3		**Round 4**

$$\int x\sin(x)\,dx$$

Evaluate

$$\int_{-1}^0 x\sin(x)\,dx$$

Give your answer correct to 3 significant figures

	Round 5		**Round 6**

Evaluate

$$\int_1^2 x^2\ln(x)\,dx$$

Give your answer in exact form.

$$\int xe^x\,dx$$

	Round 7		**Round 8**

$$\int 3xe^{-x}\,dx$$

Find the exact area enclosed by the x-axis, the curve with equation $y = xe^{2x}$ and the lines $x = 0$ and $x = 1$.

	Round 9		**Round 10**

Find the area enclosed by the x-axis, the curve $y = e^x(x-1)$ and the lines $x = -2$ and $x = -1$.
Give your answer correct to 3 significant figures.

$$\int \ln(x)\,dx$$

Race 17: Linear Combinations of sin(x) and cos(x)

AS/A2 Level	TOPICS
A2	expressing linear combinations of sin(x) and cos(x) as one function involving sine or cosine finding the maximum and minimum values of a linear combination of sin(x) and cos(x)

TEACHER'S NOTES

This activity will give students the chance to practise rewriting linear combinations of sinx and cosx as a single function of sine or cosine. There are also some questions on using this to find minimum and maximum values of the function, and questions where students can use this method to solve an equation involving a linear combination of sin(x) and cos(x).

ANSWERS

Round 1	Round 2
$5\sin(\theta + 53.1°)$	$\sqrt{29}\cos(\theta + 21.8°)$

Round 3	Round 4
$2\sin(\theta - 30.0°)$	$\sqrt{2}\cos(\theta - 45.0°)$

Round 5	Round 6
$\sqrt{2}\sin(\theta - 45.0°)$ Maximum: $\sqrt{2}$ Minimum: $-\sqrt{2}$	$\sqrt{14}\cos(\theta - 53.3°)$ Maximum: $\sqrt{14}$ Minimum: $-\sqrt{14}$

Round 7	Round 8
$\sqrt{10}\cos(\theta - 18.4°)$ $\theta = \{90.0°, 306.8°\}$	$13\sin(\theta - 67.4°)$ $\theta = \{117.4°\}$

Round 9	Round 10
$\theta = \{90°, 330°\}$	$\theta = \{24.7°, 132.7°\}$

Decimals have been rounded to 1 decimal place.

 **Round 1**	 **Round 2**
Express $$3\sin\theta + 4\cos\theta$$ in the form $R\sin(\theta+\alpha)$, where $R>0$ and $0°<\alpha<90°$.	Express $$2\sin\theta - 5\cos\theta$$ in the form $R\cos(\theta+\alpha)$, where $R>0$ and $0°<\alpha<90°$.
 **Round 3**	 **Round 4**
Express $$\sqrt{3}\sin\theta - \cos\theta$$ in the form $R\sin(\theta-\alpha)$, where $R>0$ and $0°<\alpha<90°$.	Express $$\sin\theta + \cos\theta$$ in the form $R\cos(\theta-\alpha)$, where $R>0$ and $0°<\alpha<90°$.
 **Round 5**	 **Round 6**
Express $\sin\theta - \cos\theta$ in the form $R\sin(\theta-\alpha)$, where $R>0$ and $0°<\alpha<90°$. State the minimum and maximum values of the function.	Express $3\sin\theta + \sqrt{5}\cos\theta$ in the form $R\cos(\theta-\alpha)$, where $R>0$ and $0°<\alpha<90°$. State the minimum and maximum values of the function.
 **Round 7**	 **Round 8**
Express $\sin\theta + 3\cos\theta$ in the form $R\cos(\theta-\alpha)$, where $R>0$ and $0°<\alpha<90°$. Hence solve the equation $\sin\theta + 3\cos\theta = 1$ for $0°<\theta<360°$	Express $5\sin\theta - 12\cos\theta$ in the form $R\sin(\theta+\alpha)$, where $R>0$ and $0°<\alpha<90°$. Hence solve the equation $5\sin\theta + 12\cos\theta = 10$ for $0°<\theta<180°$
 **Round 9**	 **Round 10**
Solve the equation $$\sin\theta + \sqrt{3}\cos\theta = 1$$ for $0°<\theta<360°$	Solve the equation $$5\sin\theta + \cos\theta = 3$$ for $0°<\theta<360°$

Template

	Round 1		Round 2

	Round 3		Round 4

	Round 5		Round 6

	Round 7		Round 8

	Round 9		Round 10

Template

	Round 1		Round 2
	Round 3		Round 4
	Round 5		Round 6
	Round 7		Round 8
	Round 9		Round 10

Other Stimulating Lesson Ideas from Tarquin

Mathematical Treasure Hunts *Enjoyable functional activities to enhance the curriculum.*
978 1 899618 44 6 Vivien Lucas
Most people have taken part in treasure hunts of various kinds in different social contexts. What perhaps is not generally realised is just how easy and rewarding they can be to include within the mathematics curriculum. Once the principles of organising them are understood, they can be adapted easily to the circumstances. In the book there are six complete treasure hunts, four ready to photocopy and suggestions, ideas and templates for many more.

Mathematical Team Games *Enjoyable functional activities to enhance the curriculum.*
978 1 899618 56 9 Vivien Lucas
Team Games are special mathematical puzzles and problems which produce real cooperation between the members of a team. The mathematical content is that of the normal curriculum and whether you call them games, puzzles or problems they undoubtedly offer a very positive experience at a variety of different levels. Each player only gets some of the information and so all must play a part in arriving at a solution. Sixteen tried and tested team games are provided in photocopiable form and once it is realised how well this format works, it will not be difficult to construct more for yourself.

Mathematical Merry-go round *Whole class oral activities to enhance the curriculum*
978 1 899618 59 0 Vivien Lucas
Sixteen varied and well worked out whole class activities form the heart and the purpose of this collection. The aim is to encourage everyone's active participation with the teacher directing from the front. For some of the activities the pupils have to respond verbally, for others they have to hold up coloured cards with the words 'true' or 'false' or the choices 'A', 'B', 'C' or 'D' printed on them Photocopy masters are provided for each of these cards and also of the various forms and charts needed to respond or react to the the situations being set up. Anyone looking for a way of generating enthusiasm and quick responses will find this book most useful.

Junior Mathematics Team Games *Enjoyable activities to enhance the curriculum in the upper primary school*
978 1899618 95 8 Vivien Lucas
Like its sister book, this book contains a series of games designed to present the content of the normal curriculum in co-operative problem solving activities for teams. Each player only gets some of the information required and so all must play a part in solving the problem. Topics include fractions, Shape, Multiplication and other operations, Primes and attributes of number, Data handling, Reflection, Magic Squares, Codes. An ideal photocopiable resource for the junior classroom, the mathematics club or even a school event.

Mathsheets *32 useful worksheets on a variety of mathematical topics*
978 1 899618 57 6 Dominic Turpin
The principal purpose of these photocopiable worksheets is to offer different and imaginative approaches to number work. Whether through number trails, coded messages, crossnumber puzzles, travel charts or operation trails there are calculations to do and discoveries to make. In addition there are some good ideas for work on compass directions, isometric drawing and dividing shapes into halves and quarters. Full answers are given and this collection is a handy and well-worked out resource.

The Mini Mathematical Murder Mysteries Series
Jill Whieldon
We all like to think we can solve a murder given the right clues. Here's a chance to use mathematics skills to identify "whodunit". The students are given the data or a diagram to solve a "problem" – which of four characters is a murderer. To find out, the student must solve all or most of the questions on the sheet to identify wrong answers as well as correct ones. Problems are staged, so there is an element of suspense for the individual...and racing between students to solve the mystery. Likely to take about 40 minutes but this will depend on the ability of the class to coordinate the different aspects of each task.

Junior Mini Mathematical Murder Mysteries *16 Activities to Stretch and Engage Ages 8-11*
978 1 907550 81 2

Mini Mathematical Murder Mysteries *16 Activities to Stretch and Engage Ages 11-13*
978 1 907550 10 2

More Mini Mathematical Murder Mysteries *16 Activities to Stretch and Engage Ages 13-15*
978 1 907550 25 6

These and hundreds more resources at
www.tarquingroup.com